Alice in U

Tarot Journal

Copyright: Kyoticrafts
Amazon.com/author/kyoticrafts

Notes

Card
of the
Day

Notes

*Date:*_____

Card of the Day

Date:_____

Card of the Day

Date:_____

_____

_____

Card of the Day

Date:_____

_____

_____

Card of the Day

Date:_____

_____

_____

Card of the Day

Date:_____

Card of the Day

*Date:*_____

_____

_____

_____

_____

_____

_____

_____

_____

Card of the Day   _____

                                     _____

                                     _____

                                     _____

                                     _____

                                     _____

                                     _____

                                     _____

                                     _____

Weekly Roundup

*Date:*_____

Card of the Day

*Date:*_____

_____

_____

_____

_____

_____

_____

_____

_____

Card of the Day

_____

_____

_____

_____

_____

_____

_____

_____

_____

Date:_____

Card of the Day

*Date:*_____

Card of the Day

Date:_____

Card of the Day

Date:_____

Card of the Day

*Date:*_____

_____

_____

_____

_____

_____

_____

_____

_____

_____

Card of the Day

Weekly Roundup

Notes

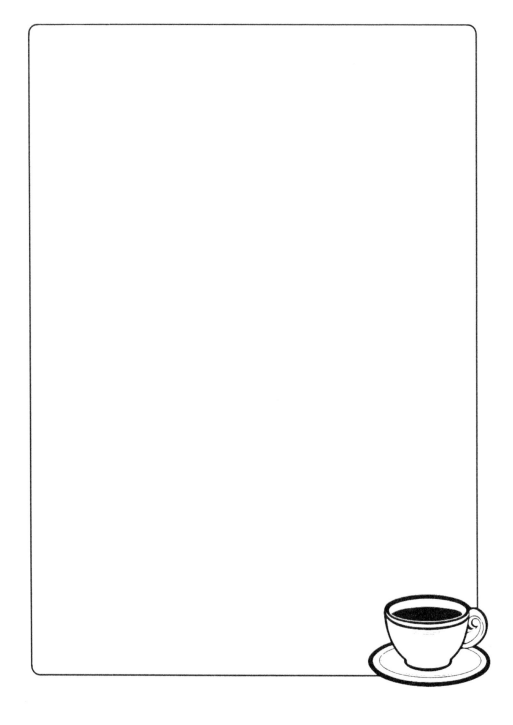

Date:_____

Card of the Day

*Date:*_____

Card of the Day

*Date:*_____

Card of the Day

*Date:*_____

_____

_____

_____

_____

_____

_____

_____

_____

_____

Card of the Day

Date: _____

Card of the Day

*Date:*_____

Card of the Day

Date:_____

Card of the Day

Weekly Roundup

Date:_____

Card of the Day

*Date:*_____

Card of the Day

*Date:*_____

_____

_____

_____

_____

_____

_____

_____

_____

Card of the Day

Date:_____

Card of the Day

Date: _____

_____

_____

_____

_____

_____

_____

_____

Card of the Day

_____

_____

_____

_____

_____

_____

_____

_____

_____

Date:_____

Card of the Day

Date:_____

Card of the Day

Weekly Roundup

Three Card Reading

Notes

3 Card Reading

Query _____ Date _____

Card Meanings

_____
_____
_____
_____

Interpretation

_____
_____
_____
_____
_____

3 Card Reading

Query _____ Date _____

Card Meanings

_____

_____

_____

_____

Interpretation

_____

_____

_____

_____

_____

3 Card Reading

Query _____ Date _____

Card Meanings

Interpretation

3 Card Reading

Query _____ Date _____

Card Meanings

_____

_____

_____

_____

Interpretation

_____

_____

_____

_____

_____

3 Card Reading

Query _____ Date _____

Card Meanings

_____

_____

_____

_____

Interpretation

_____

_____

_____

_____

_____

3 Card Reading

Query _____ Date _____

Card Meanings

Interpretation

3 Card Reading

Query _____ Date _____

Card Meanings

_____

_____

_____

Interpretation

_____

_____

_____

_____

_____

Weekly Roundup

3 Card Reading

Query _____ Date _____

Card Meanings

_____

_____

_____

Interpretation

_____

_____

_____

_____

_____

3 Card Reading

Query _____ Date _____

Card Meanings

_____
_____
_____
_____

Interpretation

_____
_____
_____
_____
_____

3 Card Reading

Query _____ Date _____

Card Meanings

_____

_____

_____

_____

Interpretation

_____

_____

_____

_____

_____

3 Card Reading

Query _____ Date _____

Card Meanings

_____
_____
_____
_____

Interpretation

_____
_____
_____
_____
_____

3 Card Reading

Query _____ Date _____

Card Meanings

_____

_____

_____

_____

Interpretation

_____

_____

_____

_____

_____

3 Card Reading

Query _____ Date _____

Card Meanings

Interpretation

3 Card Reading

Query _____ Date _____

Card Meanings

_____

_____

_____

Interpretation

_____

_____

_____

_____

_____

Weekly Roundup

Notes

3 Card Reading

Query _____ Date _____

Card Meanings

_____

_____

_____

Interpretation

_____

_____

_____

_____

_____

3 Card Reading

Query _____ Date _____

Card Meanings

_____
_____
_____

Interpretation

_____
_____
_____
_____
_____

3 Card Reading

Query _____ Date _____

Card Meanings

_____
_____
_____

Interpretation

_____
_____
_____
_____
_____

3 Card Reading

Query _____ Date _____

Card Meanings

Interpretation

3 Card Reading

Query _____ Date _____

Card Meanings

Interpretation

3 Card Reading

Query _____ Date _____

Card Meanings

Interpretation

3 Card Reading

Query _____ Date _____

Card Meanings

_____
_____
_____

Interpretation

_____
_____
_____
_____
_____

Weekly Roundup

3 Card Reading

Query _____ Date _____

Card Meanings

_____
_____
_____
_____

Interpretation

_____
_____
_____
_____
_____

3 Card Reading

Query _____ Date _____

Card Meanings

_____

_____

_____

Interpretation

_____

_____

_____

_____

_____

3 Card Reading

Query _____ Date _____

Card Meanings

Interpretation

3 Card Reading

Query _____ Date _____

Card Meanings

_____

_____

_____

_____

Interpretation

_____

_____

_____

_____

_____

3 Card Reading

Query _____ Date _____

Card Meanings

_____

_____

_____

_____

Interpretation

_____

_____

_____

_____

_____

3 Card Reading

Query _____ Date _____

Card Meanings

_____
_____
_____

Interpretation

_____
_____
_____
_____
_____

3 Card Reading

Query _____ Date _____

Card Meanings

_____

_____

_____

_____

Interpretation

_____

_____

_____

_____

_____

Weekly Roundup

Card Meanings

Notes

Major Arcana

Card	Meaning	Meaning
Fool		
Magician		
High Priestess		
Empress		
Emperor		
Hierophant		
The Lovers		
Chariot		
Strength		
Hermit		
Wheel of Fortune		

Write the meanings
of your cards on this
page as a reminder

Notes

Major Arcana

Card	Meaning	Meaning
Justice		
Hanged Man		
Death		
Temperance		
The Devil		

The Tower		
The Star		
The Moon		
The Sun		
Judgement		
The World		

Write the meanings
of your cards on this
page as a reminder

Notes

Cups

Card	Meaning	Meaning
Ace		
Two		
Three		
Four		
Five		
Six		
Seven		
Eight		
Nine		
Ten		

Write the meanings
of your cards on this
page as a reminder

Notes

Cups

Card	Meaning	Meaning
Page		
Knight		
Queen		
King		

Write the meanings
of your cards on this
page as a reminder

Notes

Wands

Card	Meaning	Meaning
Ace		
Two		
Three		
Four		
Five		
Six		
Seven		
Eight		
Nine		
Ten		

Write the meanings
of your cards on this
page as a reminder

Notes

Wands

Card	Meaning	Meaning
Page		
Knight		
Queen		
King		

Write the meanings
of your cards on this
page as a reminder

Notes

Pentacles

Card	Meaning	Meaning
Ace		
Two		
Three		
Four		
Five		
Six		
Seven		
Eight		
Nine		
Ten		

Write the meanings
of your cards on this
page as a reminder

Notes

Pentacles

Card	Meaning	Meaning
Page		
Knight		
Queen		
King		

Write the meanings
of your cards on this
page as a reminder

Notes

Swords

Card	Meaning	Meaning
Ace		
Two		
Three		
Four		
Five		
Six		
Seven		
Eight		
Nine		
Ten		

Write the meanings of your cards on this page as a reminder

Notes

Swords

Card	Meaning	Meaning
Page		
Knight		
Queen		
King		

Write the meanings
of your cards on this
page as a reminder

Notes

Notes

See my other journals on Amazon
Amazon.com/author/kyoticrafts

Printed in Great Britain
by Amazon